www.prettyawesomegift.com

Stick special photo
here

Things I Love About You!
By _____

All about you!

Your name is _____

She is _____ years old

She has _____ hair

She has _____ eyes

Her most favorite food is_____

Her most favorite drink is_____

She loves to _____

She has a beautiful _____

You look prettiest when you

I love it when you

You are funny when you

Special Portrait

You are as cool as a

Thank you for

I love when we go

You make me laugh when you

I know you love me because

I love when you say

Special Portrait

When I grow up I will buy you a

Thank you for always

Thank you for teaching me how to

Thank you for helping me to

Thank you for finding time to

I love when we play

You make me feel happy when

Amazing Picture

My best thing to do with you is

You make me smile when

Thank you for caring when

YOU ARE KIND

You are the best at

You cook the best

YOU ARE THE BEST & I LOVE YOU SO MUCH!!!

We specialize in creating personalized books for kids and adults of all ages and for all occasions.
We create a variety of interactive books such as Birthday Activity and Affirmation books to Gratitude and Prompted Journals.
Our books will help you to show your appreciation for the very special people in your life.
Visit us today at
www.prettyawesomegift.com

Made in the USA
Las Vegas, NV
26 December 2021

39369489R00031